TUDOR ENGLAND

Derek Wilson

SHIRE LIVING HISTORIES

How we worked • How we played • How we lived

Published in Great Britain in 2010 by Shire Publications
Ltd, Midland House, West Way, Botley, Oxford OX2 0PH,
United Kingdom.
44-02 23rd Street, Suite 219, Long Island City, NY 11101,
USA

E-mail: shire@shirebooks.co.uk   www.shirebooks.co.uk

A CIP catalogue record for this book is available from the
British Library.

Shire Living History no. 3 • ISBN-13: 978 0 74780 780 3

Designed by Tony Truscott Designs, UK
and typeset in Perpetua and Gill Sans.
Printed in China through Worldprint Ltd.

10 11 12 13 14   10 9 8 7 6 5 4 3 2 1

COVER IMAGE
A civic pageant (see pages 27–9).
(Painting by Graham Turner.)

ACKNOWLEDGEMENTS
AAA Collections, page 18; Bridgeman Art Library, pages 8
(bottom), 10, 14, 16, 23, 25, 32, 38, 42, 48, 59, 60, 64,
73 (left), and 73 (right); Bibliothèque Nationale/Giraudon
75 (top); British Library, pages 7, 44 (top), and 54; Corbis,
pages 11, 34, 39, and 68; Mike Cox, page 24 (top); English
Heritage Photo Library, pages 4, 13, 45, and 46–7;
exfordy, page 33; Getty Images, pages 26, 35, 40, 57, 61,
65, 66, 75; Andy Griffin, page 62; Haddon Hall, pages 41
and 44 (bottom); SLR Jester, page 19; National Portrait
Gallery, page 17; Martin Pettitt, page 22 (top); Mary
Evans Picture Library, pages 69 (bottom), and 72; Rob
Roy, pages 52, and 53 (top); Chris Selby, page 20; Lauren
Shear, page 51 (top); Shire Publications, pages 28–9; Ariel
LI Sok-Ching, page 65 (bottom); Topfoto, pages 12, 15,
31, 36 (right), 49 (top), 56, 58, 59, 69 (top left and right),
and 74; www.bountifultreasures.co.uk, page 53 (bottom).
All other images are from the author's collection.

Shire Publications is supporting the Woodland Trust, the UK's leading woodland conservation charity, by funding the dedication of trees.

CONTENTS

PREFACE

LIFE AND DEATH in the court of Henry VIII is the stuff of countless television series, feature films, lurid novels and scholarly best-sellers. Hardly surprisingly so, since the events of those years arguably shaped English history more than any equivalent period up to the Second World War; and of course the stories are so dramatic, the characters so much larger than life, and the mixture of high politics and low scandal so compelling, that no period in history is more memorable.

Yet, Tudor England was not just the goings-on of Westminster, the Tower and Hampton Court. For the vast majority of people across the country, who never once set eyes on Henry or Anne Boleyn, life went on, in some ways much as it always had, while in others profound and disruptive changes were felt. A brief period of respite after the disruption of the Wars of the Roses was followed by enforced changes to familiar religious practices and – ultimately even more important – changes to the ownership of a large proportion of the nation's land, which set in motion deep and irresistible social and economic change.

In this volume Derek Wilson, well-known author on the politics of Henry's court, now turns his attention to the reality of life in the early Tudor realm. He ranges from the changing ways people saw the world in the years when Columbus and Cabot revolutionised the globe, to the ways people tried to keep warm. He shows how the fashions of the court and ideas of the intelligentsia filtered down across society, while explaining how everyone, rich and poor, grand or humble, endured squalor, suffered painful disease and the imminence of death.

Living Histories: Tudor England is a survey of the day-to-day reality of life and death for ordinary people, rich and poor, who lived in Henry's England.

Peter Furtado
General Editor

Opposite:
The ruins of Byland Abbey in North Yorkshire reflect the dramatic change that came over England when all the hundreds of monasteries were suppressed in the 1530s, and their lands sold.

THE BYBLE IN ENGLYSHE

INTRODUCTION

SOCIETY CHANGES all the time but there are some eras in which change happens faster than others. Between 1500 and 1550 people still farmed as their forefathers had done, still took their goods to the same markets, still attended their parish churches. Most of them still lived in the same kind of houses. But they were aware that the world was changing around them, sometimes in worrying ways.

This was the age of the Renaissance when new ideas about politics, religion, art, geography, philosophy and science were challenging old assumptions. Even though only the educated few could keep up to date with the new intellectual fashions, change filtered down to all levels of society.

Consider, for example, the two maps on page 8. Less than fifty years separates them but they demonstrate the enormous strides taken in cartography during those years. When Henry VII, the first Tudor king, came to the throne in 1485 everyone believed that to the west of Ireland there lay nothing but a vast tract of unconquerable ocean separating Europe from Cathay (China). Seven years later Christopher Columbus made his famous landfall in the 'New World'. In succeeding decades mariners were exploiting newly-discovered routes to the Orient, bringing home cargoes of silks, spices, ivory and gem-stones for wealthy customers but also carrying strange tales of the peoples of other lands. It was becoming clear that people did not really understand their world at all. In 1516 Thomas More cashed in on the fascination with travellers' yarns when he wrote his best-seller, *Utopia*. In this book he described a fictitious, perfect country, in order to highlight the faults in English society and the things that needed changing.

But across the country at large life followed age-old patterns. The picture (overleaf) of men harrowing and sowing dates from around 1500, but could quite as easily have been painted a hundred years later. However, some changes *did* affect everyone – profoundly. This was

Opposite:
Title page of the Great Bible (1539). Henry VIII's decision to allow the Bible to be translated into English had a revolutionary impact because people could read it for themselves rather than relying on what the priest told them. All the people in the bottom part of the picture together shout '*Vivat Rex*', 'Long Live the King'.

Martin Waldseemüller's map of the British Isles (1522) was still based on that of the Greek geographer Ptolemy: there had been little improvement in knowledge since AD 150.

the age of the Reformation. Someone going to mass in a typical parish church at the beginning of our period would have entered a colourful and cluttered interior. Windows were bright with stained glass. Much of the wall space was painted with multicoloured frescoes. Numerous altars were laden with rich cloths, painted statues and gilded monstrances, chalices and candlesticks. The worshipper would not have expected to take any part in the service. There was a considerable gulf between clergy and laity – the priest recited his office in Latin at the altar placed at the east end of the church, keeping his back to the congregation and there was probably no sermon. Yet by the time Henry VII's grandson Edward VI died in 1553, many churches had had their walls whitewashed to obliterate the old murals and their windows now contained clear glass. Gone were the side altars, and even the high altar was likely to be an unadorned table, perhaps set sideways in the chancel. The priest no longer performed the mass as the people looked on; worshippers were provided with service books in English and were expected to recite prayers and canticles which, if they could not themselves read, they had learned by heart. The Bible was read in the vernacular and, on most Sundays, a sermon was preached.

This map by the Dutch cartographer, Abraham Ortelius (1573), indicates the enormous strides made in geography over the previous half century.

Ownership of the land on which so many people earned their livelihood had also largely changed. In 1500 there were many big estates owned by noblemen, gentlemen, bishops and monasteries (the Church owned between a quarter and a third of all the farmed land in England). Farming in most areas was 'mixed', as villages and hamlets were surrounded by fields where crops were grown and by meadows where sheep and cattle grazed. By 1550, all the monasteries had been closed down, and their lands sold to new masters with their own ideas about profitable farming. Many introduced large flocks of sheep to graze the fields that had once been ploughed for crops. This was to feed the international market for woollen cloth, England's principal export.

The great monasteries which had seemed so permanent had vanished, forcibly closed and their property sold off by command of the king. New houses appeared in their place – either country mansions erected in the latest architectural style or monastic buildings converted for their new residents. These might be ancient families who had enriched themselves by buying up church estates, or 'new men' who now acquired land for the first time, climbing the social ladder from peasant to yeoman farmer.

Above: In the reign of the Protestant Edward VI (1547–53) traditional images were stripped from churches and some Catholics left England.

Some of the most profound changes were more subtle. In the Middle Ages 'power' was largely to do with birth and territorial possession, and great noble families, like the Percies, Nevilles, Courtenays, Talbots and Howards, who could trace their ancestry back over several generations, owned vast estates, kept private bands of armed retainers and exercised control of the courts in

Previous page, bottom: This beautiful page from a sixteenth-century Italian breviary (service book) shows sowing and harrowing in the month of October. An English rural scene would not have been dissimilar.

the counties they dominated. For example, it was said that, throughout much of northern England, the people 'knew no king but a Percy'.

Theoretically all the king's subjects were equal before the law but, in practice, ordinary people found it difficult to get justice if the local lord, or someone who enjoyed his protection, had taken their property or abused them in some way. If they tried to take the case to court they would find the jury had been packed or witnesses suborned. When those at the top of the social scale resorted to violence this tended to set the tone for all relationships. A chronicler complained:

> The law is like unto a Welshman's hose,
> To each man's legs that shapen is and mete;
> So maintainers [lords' henchmen] subvert it and transpose,
> Through might it is full low laid under feet.

Lawlessness not only made life unpleasant for the underprivileged classes, it also threatened the stability of the realm and the security of the throne. This was why Henry VII confronted powerful nobles in battle and enacted laws against the keeping of private armies. Henry VIII continued the process of enforcing the authority of the state and the Tower of London was never busier than during his reign. Both Tudor kings gave the judicial system more teeth. They raised the profile of the common law (law based on study of the growing body of judicial decisions which often supported traditional customs and practices) to challenge the naked power of the nobility and the authority of the Church. By enhancing the powers of local justices of the peace (members of the gentry or rural middle classes) and appointing to administrative posts in central and local government a new breed of common lawyers (many of whom also served as Members of Parliament), they steadily changed the social balance within the country.

The biggest single innovation was the spread of printing, the most revolutionary advance in communication technology before the invention of the telephone. Movable type had been invented in the mid-fifteenth century, and printing spread rapidly by the standards of the day. By 1500 every city and sizeable town in England had at least one print workshop (in the separate kingdom of Scotland the first press did not arrive until 1508). Books, which had been expensive, handwritten luxuries now became affordable to a wider clientele. New, even revolutionary, ideas which had hitherto been confined to a small, educated elite now spread more rapidly as men (and even women) of high and low degree read books and pamphlets. This gave a great incentive to people to learn to read. But the impact of printing was not confined to the literate minority. Pictures as well as words could be produced by the presses. While church leaders commissioned aids to devotion and government agents propagated official policy, critics and satirists also ran off cheap prints intended to undermine the authority of bishops and kings.

Printing narrowed the gap between those who had and those who had not *scientia*, knowledge. Education was the great barrier which ran through society. Genuine scholars, and charlatans who pretended to arcane knowledge, were alike held in awe by their less endowed neighbours. Everyone wanted keys to those doors which promised access to the mysteries

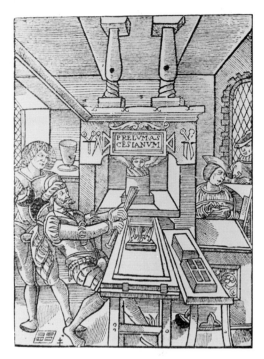

In the 1450s, Johannes Gutenberg invented a press which produced printed pages quickly and cheaply. By 1500 this had revolutionised the production of books and the spread of ideas, in England as elsewhere.

of life and death, sickness and health, poverty and riches. They turned to physicians, astrologers, alchemists, necromancers and witches. They listened eagerly to sermons. If they were able, they read books. Schools were founded where boys and, in some instances, girls could learn the basics of English and Latin grammar. Adults educated themselves, to improve their business effectiveness or to deepen their wider knowledge. One book above all revolutionised society. In 1526, the English-language New Testament (published abroad and distributed illegally) went on sale. In 1539 the whole Bible was in print, this time authorised by the king himself. Suddenly everyone who could read became his own theologian, had access to those mysteries which had hitherto eluded him. Armed with a Bible anyone could challenge the teachings of the church and the policies of the government. This was the foundation of England's emergence as a Protestant nation.

But the most insidious change of all, devastating in its impact and made worse because no-one could understand it, was inflation. Between 1500 and 1550 the cost of living trebled. The pressure on prices, wages, rents and employment is a factor which underlies much of what follows in this book.

HOME

ENGLISH ARCHITECTURE went through enormous changes in the early sixteenth century. The great Gothic period of church-building continued until around 1530, after which the progress of the Reformation put a stop to such spectacular activities. Convents and abbeys were pulled down and the incentive for private patrons to finance new or extended parish churches disappeared. Instead the rich new age of domestic architecture dawned. The first two Tudors themselves set the fashion. Henry VII built Richmond Palace and carried out extensive improvements at Windsor. Henry VIII had a positive passion for building. He owned more houses than any other monarch. Some were inherited, some confiscated, some exchanged with nobles and bishops (usually for properties of lesser value). Many of them he enlarged and modernised.

Henry VII's chapel at Westminster Abbey one of the finest example of late Gothic English architecture. The King built it between 1503 and 1512 to house his own tomb.

Opposite: Over the centuries the streets of London had become crammed with houses and shops packed close together. Areas such as Sweating's Passage were unsanitary fire hazards. Engraving from the 1790s.

Where the kings led their wealthier subjects followed. The Tudors brought to England a period of internal peace after several decades of civil war between the rival houses of Lancaster and York. During the years of unrest the leaders of society had needed castles and moated dwellings they could defend against attack. In the settled years that followed they turned their attention to making their country houses more comfortable and more impressive.

Building anew or converting former monastic dwellings provided opportunities for innovation. The first thing to change was the two-storey great hall. This had been the communal centre for the whole family in medieval times, where people ate, played indoor games and relaxed in front of the large fireplace. The heat loss in these draughty, vaulted chambers was considerable. By lowering the ceiling and creating an extra floor, owners were able to make a solar or parlour as well as extra bed-chambers. The hall was relegated to an entrance hallway with an impressive staircase that led to the upper rooms.

Henry VII built himself a new palace at Richmond in Surrey around 1500 and named it after his own hereditary title, Earl of Richmond. This painting is from 1620.

A ground-floor dining chamber completed the disappearance of the great hall. Family living was becoming more intimate, with smaller rooms designated for different functions. To overcome the lack of space for indoor exercise some owners created an upper-floor long gallery. Foreign observers were intrigued and impressed by this feature. One ambassador reported,

> Galleries are long porticoes or halls without chambers, with windows on each side, looking on gardens or rivers, the ceilings being marvellously wrought in stone [He was probably referring to elaborate plasterwork decoration] with gold; and the wainscot of carved wood representing a thousand beautiful figures.

Smaller living spaces, each with its own fireplace (Tudor houses can usually be quickly identified by the large number of chimneys) to some extent solved the problems set by the English climate, but mansions were still draughty places. The use of wood panelling stopped the cold and damp of stone or brickwork permeating the interior and this might, in turn, be covered by cloth hangings.

Wealthier owners draped the walls of their principal rooms with decorative tapestries. Most came from Flanders or were made to order by immigrant Flemish weavers but in the middle of the century the Warwickshire squire, William Sheldon, set up a factory in Bercheston to meet the growing demand. There were no carpets. Floors were strewn with sweet-smelling herbs. Items of imported 'Turkey work' (a form of knotted embroidery imitating the methods of Turkish carpets) were known in the country from the 1520s as expensive status symbols but tended to be displayed as table or dais coverings. An obvious way to keep draughts to a minimum was to glaze the windows, but glass was expensive and large sheets difficult to manufacture. Therefore, except in the homes of the wealthy, windows remained small and interiors dingy.

Although the country houses of the rich are 'untypical' of early sixteenth-century dwellings, there is good reason for devoting space to them. Their appearance all over the country made a dramatic transformation of the landscape and the innovations brought in by the rich filtered down to influence the taste of humbler men and women. At the bottom of the social scale nothing had changed. Peasants and

This fine long gallery at Packwood House, Warwickshire is a good example of the new Tudor feature, which replaced the great hall as a place for indoor exercise. The chairs and carved panelling are seventeenth-century.

15

Tapestries were hung on the walls of great houses as draught excluders but wealthy people bought highly decorative hangings (usually from Flanders) representing mythical or biblical scenes.

rural labourers still lived in thatched, timber-framed houses with earthen floors. Windows were small and closed with shutters or canvas; interiors were dark and smoky. It was still normal for the family to live on an upper floor approached by a ladder, with domestic animals occupying the space beneath. They would sleep together on straw pallets.

Between these two extremes were the houses of 'middle England' – merchants, artisans, yeoman farmers and the senior servants attached to noble households. Towns, and especially London, were becoming very crowded. Fitting more and more people into the old streets could only be achieved by adding new storeys and infill. Just how the appearance and use of a house might change is illustrated by the fate of Fitzwalter House in Old Jewry, at the heart of London's commercial centre. Once an imposing nobleman's dwelling, by 1500 it had been taken over by merchant families, and at least one mayor of London lived there. When they moved to more fashionable locales Fitzwalter House was split into tenements. It ended up as a wine tavern. Because of the demand for urban housing landlords had little incentive to improve their properties. Monastic owners had been particularly lax, as a government injunction of 1540 claimed:

> Divers and many beautiful houses of habitation…now are fallen down, decayed, and at this day remain unreedified…and some houses be feeble and very like to fall down.

London was bulging at the seams and people who either could not or did not wish to live there were moving out. The 'East End' and the 'West End' had their beginning at this time. Rich citizens built new mansions along the Strand (the main western approach to the City) with gardens running down to the river. The poor settled in an area beyond the Tower to the east described as 'a continual filthy, straight passage, with alleys of small tenements or cottages … along by the river'.

Many towns and cities were affected by changing patterns of trade. Wool was the main basis of the nation's wealth as it had been for centuries, but the export situation had changed, with profound effects on the merchant community. What foreign buyers now wanted was not the raw product but woollen cloth. The result was that a commercial city such as York, once the capital of the North, had dwindled to the status of a market town, while the Suffolk village of Lavenham where fine cloth was made, had become the thirteenth most prosperous town in England, boasting fine merchants' houses, a guildhall and other municipal buildings. The impressive half-timbered houses of the clothiers were well-built and several have survived. The owners kept up their properties well. They tiled roofs and added chimneys. They glazed their windows and decorated their exteriors with plasterwork (pargetting).

Furniture, even in wealthy households, was fairly basic. Families took their meals seated on oak benches at long oak trestle tables. They also had stools to sit on, usually made of oak or elm. The simplest chairs were known as 'backstools' and, as the name suggests, were simply stools which had been provided with a back support.

Thomas Cromwell, Henry VIII's chief minister in the 1530s, was the man behind such massive changes as the Dissolution of the Monasteries and the making of the English Bible. In this portrait by Hans Holbein note the carpet used as a table covering to the left of the picture and the patterned cloth on the wall.

EARL OF ESSEX.

This bedchamber in a modest home shows a four-poster for the householder and his wife and a truckle bed for children.

There was no upholstered furniture. Some people owned 'armed chairs' which had padded arms and cushioned seats for extra comfort. In order to be really cosy on a winter's evening it was important to counteract draughts. This was achieved by the use of high-backed settles. Beds also had to keep the cold out. Wainscot beds were set in the wall and had curtains that could be drawn across at night, but larger houses could accommodate four-posters, which had high headboards and curtains on the other three sides. Most items that needed to be stored, from clothes and linen to documents and valuables, were kept in coffers, usually made of oak. The most secure chests were of iron or were iron-bound. The best ones, with complicated locking devices, came from Germany. Food obviously could not be stored in such closed containers, but was kept in cupboards, either free-standing or attached to a wall, with pierced fronts. In fashionable homes where much feasting took place, food and gold or silver plate was set out on open cupboards called 'buffets'.

Towns had communal wells and fountains fed by conduits from nearby water courses. In the country water usually had to be fetched from rivers. Most wives and servants did their household laundry at the riverside. Water could not be used for flushing away human waste, which went straight into indoor or outdoor latrines cleaned out periodically by 'gong farmers'. Because of the stench of their jobs they had to work at night, carrying their foul-smelling wagonloads to sites well away from human habitation.

One more pleasant feature of Tudor domestic life that was new was the garden. Hitherto any land attached to a house had been used for utilitarian purposes, growing the herbs, vegetables and fruit needed by the household. This remained important but the Renaissance concept of the pleasure garden had arrived from Italy and France by the mid-1500s. Formal beds in geometrical patterns bordered by low hedges of lavender or box and interspersed with grassed or gravel walks were the height of fashion and wealthy patrons employed what were, in effect, 'garden architects', for the overriding principle was that the garden should mirror the design of the house.

Gardens as we know them were invented by the Tudors. Paths, flower beds and hedges were laid out in geometrical patterns. This example is from Malmesbury Abbey, where the garden has now been replanted in Tudor style.

NEIGHBOURHOOD

Few people in early Tudor England got about very much. Communities were tight-knit and well spread out. A trip to the nearest market town might involve a journey on foot, on horseback or by wagon of a few hours. Those who worked the land or engaged in local trade seldom had the time or the need to travel far, as the needs of villagers were catered for by a carter who would go to market with a list of what his neighbours needed and buy on their behalf. Sometimes people made an effort to go on a journey – perhaps for a pilgrimage or to appear in a court case at the county assize – but, apart from such special occasions, men and women found most of what they wanted locally. Fortunately for historians, though, there was one man who travelled extensively throughout the land, making careful notes as he went. This was John Leland, who was commissioned by Henry VIII to compile a record of England's towns and villages. Leland's *Itinerary in England and Wales* was compiled between 1535 and 1543.

The parish church was the centre of local life. It was the focal point not only of religious rituals but also local celebrations and even business. During the first thirty years of the century more churches were built or enlarged than at any other time. Lavenham, in Suffolk, was a village which had grown rich on the woollen cloth trade. In 1485, the lord of the manor, the Earl of Oxford, and the wealthy merchant, Thomas Spryng, organised the building of a new church to celebrate the victory of Henry VII at the Battle of Bosworth. Their magnificent achievement was completed in 1530. At about the same time, the parishioners of St James, Louth, in Lincolnshire, erected a fine new spire on their church tower which soared to 96 metres and is today one of the most famous spires in England. People were very proud of their churches and devoted much money and effort to making them beautiful. A popular way of raising funds was 'church ales'. A strong brew of ale would be made and sold and folk would

Opposite:
The impressive spire of Louth church. Parishioners were so proud of it that in 1536, when they heard a rumour that Henry VIII was going to take away their treasures, they started a rebellion.

The Earl of Oxford, who was responsible for the building of Lavenham church in about 1530, made sure that his heraldic device, the boar, was featured prominently in the spandrels over the entrance.

Chichester, like many English towns and cities, had changed little throughout the Middle Ages. It was still contained within its ancient walls. Besides its cathedral it boasted nine churches and a friary.

gather for drinking, dancing and general merrymaking. An inscription can still be seen on a gallery in South Tawton church, Devon: 'With good ale was this work made'.

Within the community of town or village, people often banded together in smaller communities for mutual support and to undertake common tasks. Such associations were known as 'guilds' and took various forms. Every trade had its guild, which was a form of closed shop which protected its members from competition from newcomers or from non-members. At a higher level came the powerful merchant guild, an association of the leading men of the town. In effect, they often constituted the town council. But the basic guild, from which the others may have developed, had a specific religious function. Every church contained several altars or shrines, as well as the main, or high, altar, each

10 Chichester in the early seventeenth century, still influenced by the Roman plan (Speed)

CHICHESTER

A	S. Maryenes	I	S. Peters	R	East Gate
B	The Pallant	K	Peradise	S	S. Pancras
C	Pallant ffreet	L	East lane	T	S. Bartholme
D	Black fryers	M	Crumlane	V	S quiery Bridg.
E	S. Andrews	N	wefst lane	W	South Gate
F	S. Maryes Hofp.	O	S². Touflos	X	North Gate
G	Grayfryers	P	S. Richards ruin		
H	The Pallice	Q	Our Ladyes chap.		

dedicated to a specific saint. These needed to be looked after; altar furnishings had to be found, statues painted. Candles and lamps had to be provided and kept burning, priests hired to say masses. This was where the guild came in. Its members undertook those tasks and raised the necessary funds. Money came directly from guild members, usually in the form of bequests; a man would leave a specific sum or parcel of land in his will and the income from it would maintain the altar. The legacy involved payment for regular masses to be recited for the benefactor's soul. His living brethren would ensure that his wishes were met and that guild funds were carefully administered. They might have to assist with funeral expenses or help members who were in difficulties, a necessary practice at a time when there was no national system of social security and the care of the poor and needy was the responsibility of the parish.

Some guilds and parishes were able to supplement their income from pilgrimage. It was not only major national shrines like Canterbury or Walsingham which attracted visitors eager to gaze on images of the saints or the reliquaries which, supposedly, contained fragments of bone, clothing or items which had actually had physical contact with long-dead holy men and women. St Day was a tiny hamlet near the Cornish town of Redruth but its church boasted an impressive painting of the Holy Trinity to which visitors flocked.

One of the most spectacular of the East Anglian 'wool churches' is at Long Melford, Suffolk. Its three-gabled lady chapel is unique.

23

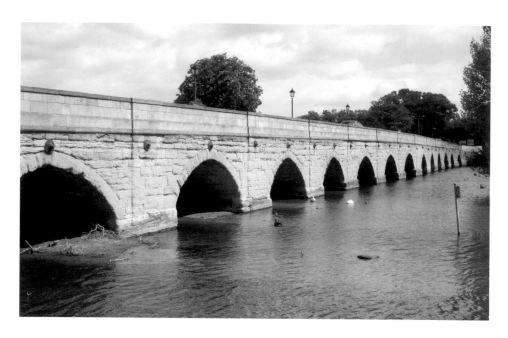

Sir Hugh Clopton, once a Lord Mayor of London, left money to his native Stratford-upon-Avon for the building of an impressive bridge to replace the ford which travellers had had to use before.

According to a sixteenth-century chronicler, 'the resort was so great as it made the people of the country bring all kind of provision [so] that it grew to a kind of market [centre]'.

The prosperous Midlands town of Stratford-upon-Avon was very different from St Day in far-off Cornwall, but here too life was largely regulated by a guild. Its prominent townsmen were united in a brotherhood called the Guild of the Holy Cross. They had their own chapel, built in the late fifteenth century, where no fewer than five priests were employed to say masses continually for the souls of departed guild members and to serve as teachers of local children.

Rural depopulation was a growing problem. Changing patterns of agriculture forced whole families to leave their homes in search of a better life.

The money to pay them came from bequests in the form of cash or land which increased from generation to generation. The guildsmen were involved in administering local charities, regulating the operation of the market and maintaining the fabric of the church as well as other amenities. The variety of their responsibilities is illustrated by the will of their most famous member, Sir Hugh Clopton, who died in 1496. He left money for the refurbishment of the parish church and the guild chapel, the building of a new bridge, for providing dowries for poor Stratford maidens and for sending boys to the universities of Oxford and Cambridge. All this had to be administered by his brethren of the Holy Cross. Similar guilds in other towns maintained almshouses and hospitals. It was exacting work. According to Leland, when Geoffrey Barber provided for the building of a bridge at Culham, Oxfordshire, 'There wrought that summer 300 men on the bridge'.

Sadly, no amount of charity was able to keep pace with the growing problem of rural poverty.

> Poor folk for bread cry and weep.
> Towns pulled down to pasture sheep.

Enclosure (the requisitioning and fencing of communal ploughlands for grazing flocks of sheep belonging to the gentry) was only one cause of rural depopulation. Inflation pushed up rents. Changes of land ownership or land use often led to long-established tenants being turned out. Sometimes whole hamlets and even villages were razed by landlords forced by economic pressure to make their estates pay. Individuals and whole families found themselves dispossessed and obliged to beg for their bread. In increasing numbers they took to the road in search of seasonal work. Some resorted to crime. Just how serious the problem was is revealed by a statute of 1531, which decreed that any 'able-bodied vagabond or idle person' was to be:

Penalties for vagabondage were harsh because the government feared that jobless, wandering men would swell the criminal class.

> Tied to the end of a cart naked and beaten with whips throughout the town ... till his body be bloody ... And after such punishment ... [he] shall be enjoined upon his oath to return forthwith ... to the place where he was born or where he last dwelled ... and there put himself to labour like as a true man oweth to do.

The law assumed that responsibility for maintaining order and keeping crime off the streets lay with the local authorities. In *Utopia* Thomas More complained at the harshness and pointlessness of punishing men for falling into poverty. 'Rather provision should have been made,' he wrote, 'whereby there were some means whereby they might get a living.' That was easier said than done.

The authorities, though, thought in terms of deterrence rather than prevention. Punishment for a wide range of crimes was public on the principle that, since the community had been offended, the community should see justice done. Every population centre had its pillory, stocks, cucking-stool and gibbet. The pillory and stocks were wooden contrivances to which the guilty were fastened so that their neighbours could express their disapproval by hurling abuse or garbage at them. A variant of this was a stake to which the miscreant was chained by means of rings round his neck and feet. The cucking-

Every village in Tudor England, like this one in Rutland, had its place for the punishment of offenders. The stocks and whipping post were at the centre of community life – a permanent reminder to people to behave themselves.

stool was a chair sometimes situated beside the local river or pond. Once fixed into it, the offender might be left to face the indignation of the people or ducked in the water (hence the variant form 'ducking stool'). This treatment seems to have had little connection with any judicial process. Anyone identified as a foul-mouthed woman or a fraudulent tradesman might be grabbed by a mob and given a taste of the 'stool'. The gibbet was a much more serious affair. It stood usually just outside the town and consisted of a chain or cage suspended from a beam. The bodies of executed criminals were displayed on gibbets and frequently left there until they had almost completely decayed. In 1537 more than seventy rebels were hanged in the northern shires following the Pilgrimage of Grace (the widespread rebellion against Henry VIII's religious policies), and the King ordered that their bodies be hung from gibbets, trees and church steeples as a warning. He was furious when the relatives of several of the dead men came secretly to recover the bodies and give them decent burial.

With such common sights as this it is obvious that life in England's towns and villages was what we might call 'basic'. The people lived very close to death, participated in violent reprisals against offenders and had an unsophisticated attitude towards crime and punishment. But community life had its pleasanter side. Venting their indignation on evildoers was only one of several forms of diversion.

The cycle of church festivals brought events which were both familiar and impressive. As soon as Christmas was over the new year began in rural parishes with Plough Sunday, when parishioners paraded round the village and ended up in the church for a service of blessing the plough. As Easter approached another procession was made to the church on Palm Sunday. This time it was the consecrated host which was escorted thither, to represent Christ's entry to Jerusalem. In a town like Long Melford, Suffolk, the ritual was very elaborate, involving clergy in colourful copes, choirboys singing from a specially-erected platform and the scattering of flowers over the congregation. So the year went on, each feast and saint's day being marked with rituals in which most people were involved.

It is not difficult to imagine the shock which was widely felt in 1547, when the government ordered churchwardens to,

> Take away ... and destroy all shrines, covering of shrines, candlesticks ... pictures, paintings and all other monument of feigned miracles, idolatry and superstition, so that there remain no memory of the same in walls, glass windows, or elsewhere within their churches ...

Overleaf: Pageants marking saints days and other important events were a mix of religious, traditional legends and civic pride. The green man and the hobby horse were ancient symbols of fertility. Holy relics were paraded under canopies and town dignitaries took pride of place in the procession. (Painting by Graham Turner.)

WORK

'WHORESON LOMBARDS! You rejoice and laugh! By the mass, we will one day have a day at you!' This threat was made by a senior member of the Mercers' Company, and what made him angry was that foreign traders, settled outside the London city limits and not subject to its commercial regulations, were undercutting the native merchants. On May Day in 1517 the ill-feeling boiled over in a night of terrifying riot and looting. Every trade had its own guild which governed prices, wages, quality control, training of apprentices and everything to do with the interests of its members. In London there were more than a hundred such guilds, or livery companies as they were called. Goldsmiths, haberdashers, ironmongers, vintners, skinners and other trades all had their own organisations. Any young man setting out to be his own boss had a long road ahead of him.

First he had to serve an apprenticeship of, probably, seven years. He lived with his master's family while he learned his craft and was treated as a servant. The next stage was that of journeyman, a paid employee, trusted to work without close supervision. Only when he had spent several years in this capacity could he apply to the council of his livery company, with specimens of his work or proof of his competence, in the hope of being admitted as a master with the right to set up his own shop.

The Worshipful Company of Goldsmiths regulated the superb work produced by London craftsmen. This silver gilt and crystal goblet, a typically ornate piece of work, was presented to the Lord Mayor in 1558.

Opposite:
This memorial brass to the wealthy Ipswich clothier Thomas Pownder (d. 1525) and his family displays Pownder's wool mark and his armorial bearings, suggesting his commercial standing was as important to him as his impressive ancestry.

In 1547 the boy king, Edward VI, processed through London on the eve of his coronation. Here he is shown passing along Cheapside. Note the city's tightly packed houses.

In London and other major centres each craft was located in its own part of the city. The capital's goldsmiths were, inevitably, to be found in the smartest street, Cheapside. One Venetian visitor was so impressed with the fifty-two shops there that he described them as 'so rich and full of silver vessels, great and small,' as to outdo 'all the shops in Milan, Rome, Venice and Florence put together'. One cannot help suspecting that this was something of a traveller's tale. The fishmongers, not surprisingly, had their premises alongside the Thames. Riverine breezes did something to disperse the smell of their stalls on Fish Wharf and Fish Street. The armourers, a pretty noisy bunch, were to be found close by the city's northern wall, around Moorgate. Each company had its own guild hall, where feasts and ceremonies were held and where records were kept. These were among the most prestigious buildings in London, as befitted the importance of the merchant companies upon which the prosperity of the capital in large measure rested.

The guildmasters were the millionaires of the day. It was from among their ranks that the city's aldermen were elected and many of them belonged to the Merchant Adventurers' Company. These were the Tudor equivalent of monopolistic fat cats, the nation's 'bankers', the plutocrats to whom other merchants, nobles and even kings turned when they wanted to borrow money. Their income came from the tight control they exercised over trade at an international level. The Merchant Adventurers enjoyed the lion's share of all trade between London and northern Europe. To all intents and purposes this meant the trade in woollen cloth.

It was a cut-throat and exploitative business. 'The rich men, the clothiers, be concluded and agreed among themselves to hold and pay one price for weaving, which price is too little to sustain households upon, working night and day, holiday and weekday, and many weavers are therefore reduced to the position of servants'. This was a complaint made in the 1530s by those at the bottom end of the manufacturing process. Textile production was a cottage industry. Wool was turned into various grades of cloth by shearers, carders, spinners, weavers, fullers and dyers working from home. Those in charge of the process were the regional 'clothiers', men like Thomas Spryng of Lavenham. They kept their costs down by paying their workers as little as possible – hence the weavers' complaint. But the clothiers, in their turn, were under pressure because they had to deal with the monopolists of the Merchant Adventurers' Company. They despatched the bales of finished cloth to London by packhorse.

Cloth merchants were the cream of East Anglian society. Fine half-timbered houses such as Paycocke's House at Coggeshall proclaimed their wealth and status.

Dunster in Somerset was one of the small towns which prospered from the trade in woollen cloth. Merchants gathered in the octagonal Tudor 'yarn market' to do their deals.

Once unloaded at Bakewell Hall in Basinghall Street the clothiers had to accept the price fixed by the buyers. The situation was made worse when some of the London men, after the Dissolution of the Monasteries in the 1530s, bought their own sheep runs and were thus able to dominate the whole process, cutting out the regional middle men.

Of course, not all land was given over to pasturing sheep. Every village practised a mixed economy. The peasant and yeoman farmers kept cows, sheep, goats, chickens and geese. They planted (with regional variations) wheat, barley, peas, oats and rye. Some cottagers grew flax for the production of linen, in a garth or garden plot beside the house. They took their grain to the local mill for grinding. Mills, powered by water or wind, were in most cases owned by the lord of the manor, and since there was nowhere else the producers could obtain their flour, the miller could set his own price, just as the landowner could demand whatever rent he wanted from the miller. It is not surprising that millers tended to have a poor reputation. The term 'miller's thumb' had long been used to describe any shady deal.

It referred to the miller's alleged practice of putting his thumb on the balance when weighing out the grain.

The medieval open-field system of working the arable acreage was finally disappearing in favour of one more readily adaptable to local conditions and demands. Under the old system, which Leland called 'champion', all villagers worked by rotation, strips in three common fields and paid the landlord in cash or kind. By 1500 most peasants had begun to rationalise land use. Fields were made larger and worked by communal endeavour, thus cutting the wastage of land between the strips. It was not only rich landlords who practised enclosure. At Nassington, Northamptonshire, 52 cottagers owned 1,200 sheep. When the Dissolution of the Monasteries suddenly brought large areas of land onto the open market, many enterprising peasants were able to buy their plots and gradually work their way up into the yeoman class.

Country people had several ways of augmenting the income they gained from their produce. Animals were sources not only of meat, wool and dung (for fertiliser), but also provided hides for making into jerkins, belts and boots, and bones which, on days when poor weather prevented outdoor work, could be fashioned into bobbins, needles, toys, dice and small tools.

They could also add to their own food supply by fishing and trapping. Much of the best open land was reserved for hunting by the king, nobles and abbots but on the 'common' land peasants might take coneys (rabbits) and wildfowl. In some places this was a rich source of food supplement. It was reported that in the fenland around the Wash 'above three thousand mallards and other fowls of the like kind' were taken in one August. But there were many areas where such pickings were meagre. In years of poor harvest, people struggled to subsist. Then the temptation was strong to venture onto forbidden land and poach game preserved for the lord and his wealthy guests. But the risk was great: poaching was punishable by death.

Some places, such as the Weald of Kent or the Forest of Dean, where furnaces were used to smelt iron, saw a steady disappearance of woodland. This was a situation which worried many people.

> ... if the iron mills be suffered to continue there will not only be such scarcity of timber that there will not be [enough] to build in the parts near them either houses, watermills or windmills, bridges, sluices, ships ... but also the towns of Hastings and Rye ... shall not be able to have in the country nigh by reason of the iron mills timber sufficient to maintain their piers and jetties.

So reported a royal commission in 1548. Ironworking had been carried on in these areas from time out of mind but now production methods were changing. Hitherto the charcoal needed for the smelting process had been produced by groups of itinerant charcoal burners who were working largely to meet the needs of local

The money which lubricated commerce was made in mints around the country, of which the most important was at the Tower of London. The picture shows gold or silver being smelted, weighed out and struck into coins.

blacksmiths and tool makers. But Henry VIII's wars created a much increased demand for cannon, handguns and other military materiel. The iron industry responded by developing the more efficient blast furnace. The cost of this expensive equipment took control away from the traditional workers and placed it in the hands of wealthy capitalists and estate owners such as Sir William Sidney of Penshurst in Kent, who bought the site of the Cistercian monastery of Robertsbridge, Sussex and created a foundry there.

England's industrial base was still small but it was varied and growing. The shortage of firewood created a demand for coal. 'Sea coal' was so called because it was brought to London and the South-East by coastal vessels from open cast mines in Durham and Northumberland. Tin was produced in Devon and Cornwall and was vital for the production of pewter and bell metal. England was Europe's leading producer of lead and could scarcely produce enough to supply the demand at home and abroad created by the spate of house and church building. In all these undertakings the commercial pattern was the same: as with the textile industry power and wealth were being concentrated in fewer and fewer hands. English capitalism was emerging.

A gold sovereign of the final years of Henry VII's reign.

Opposite: Henry VIII spent several years in foreign wars. This provided work for armourers, who as here produced finely crafted work as well as run-of-the-mill body protection, and greatly boosted the English iron industry.

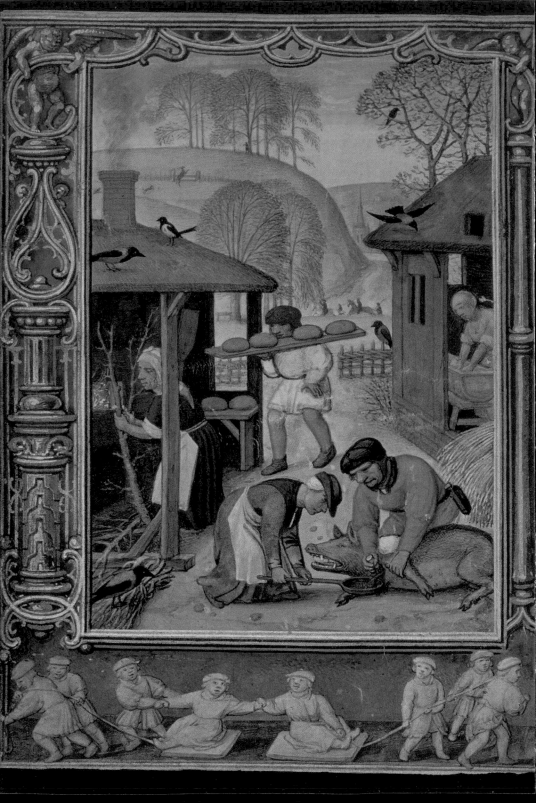

FOOD

'**B**ETTER IS A MESS OF POTTAGE with love than a fat ox with evil will.' So declared the Matthew's Bible, one of the first vernacular Bibles, published in 1537. In so doing it brought together the two culinary extremes known to Tudor people. Many a poor man never got to taste a 'fat ox'. Pottage, on the other hand, was the Englishman's basic form of nourishment. 'Pottage is not so much used in all Christendom as it is used in England', wrote 'Merry Andrew', Dr Andrew Boorde, the earliest exponent of healthy eating, in his *Compendious regyment or a dietary of helth* (1542). Boorde described pottage as meat stock to which oatmeal, herbs and salt were added but there was no precise recipe for this dish. It was a stockpot, kept heated on most hearths, to which vegetables, herbs and any scraps might be added. In many homes such a pot was innocent of all connection with meat; it was merely a thick vegetable stew.

Andrew Boorde (1490–1549) – one-time friar, traveller, author, physician and bon-viveur – was one of the 'celebrities' of the age. In his books he analysed the effects of food, housing and personal habits on health. He profited little from his own advice and died in the Fleet prison.

The diet of most English people was restricted by three things – income, problems of preserving and religious law. Harvest yield was fundamental to the prosperity of the country as a whole and, particularly, to those who lived directly off the land. Yields fluctuated wildly throughout the early Tudor period. For most of the time they were adequate but a run of poor harvests, such as those of 1500–03, 1519–21, 1527–9 and 1549–51, caused real misery. Corn prices rocketed. In 1521 they hit a 200-year high. Farmers were faced with a bitter dilemma. Every year they kept back a proportion of the crop for the following season's planting. With the larder emptying, should

Opposite:
This page from a calendar of the 1520s shows typical events of December. A pig is slaughtered to provide winter meat. Bread is baked, probably in a communal oven.

Larger households often brewed their own ale. Here we see in the background, the malt 'mash' and water being mixed. In the centre it is being cooled, before being stored in barrels (foreground).

they sell some of their seed corn in order to keep body and soul together or tighten their belts in the hope of a better crop the following year? Distress could provoke social upheaval. In 1528 several men were hanged in Norwich and Great Yarmouth. Their crime? Waylaying the wagons of corn-chandlers who were selling their grain elsewhere when it was desperately short locally. All this happened, as we have seen, when several landlords were turning over arable land to pasture, thus exacerbating the problem.

Fresh food could only be eaten in season by most people. Farmers living on or near the subsistence level could not afford hay or grain to feed all their beasts through the winter. Therefore, they had to slaughter in the autumn when the meadows had been grazed down and preserve the meat by salting or smoking. It was customary to keep a pig for household needs. Properly cured and carefully eked out, this could provide enough ham and bacon to feed an average sized family at least until spring. If the household was lucky enough it would have access to other sources of flesh. Any creature that could be legally trapped or shot with bow and arrow was, literally, 'fair game'. Rabbits, hares, wildfowl and almost every kind of bird were potential supplements to the otherwise dreary diet. Wading birds might be taken on the village pond or stream and rabbits in a nearby cony-garth (warren). Children were often taught to trap pigeons, rooks or even sparrows.

The Church designated certain 'days of abstinence'. On Fridays and throughout Lent people were forbidden to eat meat. This was intended as a spiritual exercise but it did make practical sense for the poorer members of society. In the barren months of winter it was prudent to conserve as much salted meat as possible for consumption throughout the spring planting season, before fresh produce once more became available in summer. Eggs were also prohibited for the forty days of Lent (hence the practice of feasting on pancakes on Shrove Tuesday, the day before the beginning of Lent) but this was, in any case, the time of year when chickens and geese were laying few. Non-observance of the Lenten fast became a protest indulged in by some Protestants in Henry VIII's reign. Bishops actually sent snoopers around to see what people were eating in the hope of sniffing out heretics.

Bread was the staple food for many people but it took various forms. The cheapest was horse bread, made from ground beans. As the name suggests, it was used as an animal foodstuff, though there were times when the poorest members of society were driven to subsisting on it. Maslin was the basic food of the majority. It was greyish in colour and made from mixed grain, usually wheat and rye. White (or, more accurately, yellowish) bread (manchet), baked from pure wheat flour, was very expensive and served only in the very best households. Since leavened bread requires an oven in which temperature can be controlled and sustained and since most householders cooked on open fires, most bread was unleavened. Yeasted loaves could be bought at markets and in town shops. It was quite usual for housewives to mix their own dough and take it to the professional baker to be finished in his oven.

Water was not the staple of life we regard it as today. This was because it was difficult for most people to obtain an unpolluted supply. In the country people collected their water from wells and streams. Most towns had, thanks to municipal action and private charity, supplies of piped water. Lead pipes brought the water from springs and rivers to 'cisterns' or 'conduits' from which citizens could draw for their domestic needs. In 1500 London had about twenty such public outlets. Private supply was virtually unknown. In 1515, the wealthy London merchant, John Fleming had a pipe laid to his own house but, in response, he had to agree to his own spring outside the city being connected to the municipal supply. Most water was used for animals and for washing and cooking rather than drinking, for, as Boorde observed, 'water is not wholesome sole by itself'.

Everyone, from childhood up, drank ale. It was home-brewed in all but the humblest cottages and appeared in various strengths. It was considered to be very

Preparation of sweet meats, cakes, fruit dishes and pies for a Henrician banquet, as recreated by the Tudor Group of re-enactors at Haddon Hall.

This nineteenth-century painting of a Tudor kitchen, at Cotehele, Cornwall, shows the cauldrons and implements used for boiling and roasting. Note the haunches of salted and dried meat as well as utensils of pottery and pewter.

much an Englishman's drink, corresponding to wine, which was drunk in France and beer, the popular beverage of Germany and the Low Countries. Throughout our period, beer – which is, simply stated, ale to which hops have been added – was becoming popular. Boorde deplored this importation of a degenerate, foreign habit: 'it killeth them which be troubled with the colic and the stone and the strangulation [hernia]…it doth make a man fat and doth inflate the belly'. Nevertheless, beer gained in popularity, not only because of its flavour, but also because hops had a preservative effect. Ale went off after a few days, which meant that it had to be brewed continuously. Under the right conditions beer, by contrast, could be kept for a year or longer. The brewing of ale from barley was a complex and time-consuming business but the equipment necessary and the raw material were not expensive. For this reason many poor people made ale for sale to their neighbours and passing travellers. The alehouse was the cheapest wayside resting place on most roads.

Such establishments were therefore viewed with suspicion by the authorities who considered them (often with good reason) as haunts of thieves and meeting places of men with seditious intent. Other features which made ale-brewing commercially attractive were that two or three brews of varying strengths could be drawn off the 'mash' (the mixture of ground malt with water) and that the residue could then be fed to the household pigs.

Nothing was wasted in the best-regulated household. For example, offal made its appearance in 'pumps', balls of chopped meat mixed with herbs and (in richer homes) imported spices and raisins. Stewed giblets formed the basis of a dish known, unappetisingly, as 'garbage'. Mixed with breadcrumbs and spices it could be quite palatable. Cooks had to use their ingenuity in combining meat scraps with nuts, eggs, onions, parsley, thyme, mint, saffron and other ingredients to cover the taste of tainted meat and to make it go further. They had at their disposal various other foodstuffs which they produced themselves or bought in town or market. Apples, pears, plums, quinces and even peaches were grown in England. Wild berries could also be collected. Cardinal Wolsey is credited with inventing the combination of strawberries and cream. Honey was very popular and of such good quality that it was actually exported in considerable quantities. In Wales it became the basis of a particularly potent drink, metheglin. Sir Thomas Elyot wrote that it was, 'by reason of hot herbs boiled with honey, hotter than mead'. Alcoholic drinks other than ale and beer tended to be regional specialities. Mead, cider and perry had not spread far from their traditional West Country homelands by 1550.

The items that bulked up the diet of most people were fish and cheese. Fishing was very important to townsmen and villagers, especially during Lent. When, in 1527, the monks of Tavistock Abbey erected a weir on the river running through their grounds, the locals were outraged because it interfered with their fishing rights. A gang of 300 men descended upon the offending structure and destroyed it. Milk was not as plentiful as we might think because cows had not yet been bred to produce large yields. Most of what was left after they had finished suckling went to make cheese and butter. Whey — the

Courtier and diplomat Sir Thomas Elyot wrote on a variety of topics and in his *Castel of Helth* (1534) he analysed common ailments and stressed the importance of diet.

43

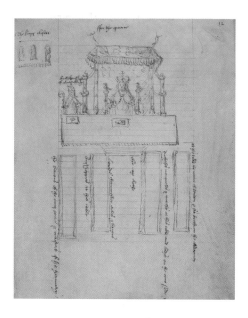

In 1533 Henry VIII's second wife, Ann Boleyn, was crowned. This drawing shows the seating plan for her coronation banquet. The queen, under a canopy, presides at top table over various dignitaries lower down the hall.

residue from the cheese-making process — was drunk. Again, nothing went to waste. All this suggests that, in a good year, the average English family enjoyed a reasonably varied diet.

Food has always been a status symbol: few people even today are served on a regular basis with dishes involving foie gras, truffles and other rare delicacies washed down with vintage claret. Five hundred years ago the distinction between the table fare of the top people and everyone else was much more marked. Government was concerned to prevent people getting 'above their station' and actually legislated the quantity and quality of dishes that might be served at the tables of various social ranks (sumptuary laws). Thus, in 1517, it was decreed that for a single course, a cardinal and his guests might enjoy nine dishes, a duke seven, an abbot six, and so on. Accounts of Tudor banquets served at the courts of Henry VIII, Cardinal Wolsey and other dignitaries set the mind boggling. First would come a salad of fresh, raw and cooked vegetables. This was followed with the first course

For a feast, food would often be decorated with heraldic or other graphic motifs. From Haddon Hall.

The simple kitchen of Yarmouth Castle in the Isle of Wight, one of a chain of defensive fortresses built along the south coast by Henry VIII.

proper – a cavalcade of roast and boiled meats and fish, all elaborately presented (e.g. a peacock would have its meat removed, cooked and stuffed back inside the carcase and served with its brilliant feathers displayed) and accompanied by a variety of sauces. The host would be sure to impress his guests by including the latest rare and exotic comestibles imported from abroad. These delicacies were interspersed with sweet dishes. When that had been cleared a similar mixed course followed including tarts, custards, pies, jellies and sugar and marchpane (marzipan) confections of architectural intricacy. Host and guests finally 'wound down' with a 'voider' course of cheese, nuts and hippocras (sweet wine flavoured and perfumed with spices).

If any yeoman farmer had ever been admitted as a witness to such gastronomic riches, he might have concluded, as he returned to his simple routine of breakfast (6 a.m.), dinner (11 a.m.) and supper (5 p.m.) that he had been transported to some fairy kingdom.

Overleaf:
The kitchen of a large household was a hot, busy, noisy place and not particularly clean. Many people were employed producing the numerous dishes presented at a banquet. (Painting by Ivan Lapper.)

45

STYLE

TODAY we have fairly clear ideas about what clothing is appropriate for different people and situations. The suit and tie, once obligatory for men working in offices, is less common. A quarter of a century ago women would have worn a dress or skirt and blouse to work, but many now turn up in jeans. Older folk tend to dress more formally than the young, and in broad terms modern dress sense is determined by age.

'The Ambassadors' by Holbein shows two stylish and wealthy men in 1533, surrounded by objects relating to their cultural and intellectual sophistication. On the left is the French ambassador to London, and on the right a figure presumed to be Georges de Selve, Bishop of Lavaur. In the foreground is an anamorphic skull; when the painting was placed at the top of a staircase, the skull became visible as the viewer approached it.

In the early sixteenth century codes were much stricter and were based, not on age, but on social status. Even those who could afford to wear jewellery and clothes of silk and velvet were forbidden by law to do so unless they were of noble or gentle rank. The church taught that God had appointed every person to a particular station in life and the government chose to discourage people from visibly climbing above their class. As a result, anyone could immediately 'place' a stranger or identify his position in society, by his attire. Some crooks took advantage of this, as is shown by the misadventure of a visitor to London around the middle of the century. He was in St Paul's Cathedral admiring the monuments and richly-dressed altars, when he fell into conversation with a handsome man clad in silks and adorned with jewelled rings. Flattered that such an obviously important person should take notice of him, he was delighted when his new 'friend' invited him to dinner. They were

Peasant costume and demeanour were very different from those of their 'betters', as is shown by these merrymakers at a fair in Germany; an English scene would probably not have been very different.

Dress was a vital tool for confidence tricksters. Nicholas Jennings, a notorious con-man, could pose as either a gentleman or a beggar in the 1550s and 1560s.

The pedlar was one of the few itinerants who formed a link between court, city and remote villages. He could easily persuade country folk that his wares represented the latest fashions.

joined at the meal by several of his host's acquaintances. Afterwards cards were produced and the naïve newcomer did not escape until he had been fleeced of everything he possessed. This was far from being an isolated event. Clearly there were good reasons for trying to make social distinctions obvious.

Even so, it was difficult to enforce dress codes by law. People naturally wanted to ape their betters and as they acquired disposable income they spent some of it on finery. Fashions filtered down through society. Women in villages distant from the capital were dependent on travelling peddlers who brought them ribbons, kerchiefs and trinkets, assuring them that their stock represented the very latest court fashions. But by 1550 the growing demand for fashionable clothes had led some entrepreneurs to set up shops in towns across the land. One such was James Backhouse, a shopkeeper of Kirkby Lonsdale, Westmorland. When he died early in Elizabeth's reign after several years in business, he left stock that included Spanish silks, French garters, Norwich lace, Oxford gloves and Turkey-work purses. By this time, the prevailing mood was very much 'If you've got it flaunt it' and, since there were few other material possessions to spend money on, people tended to wear their fortunes on their backs. By the middle of the century people were complaining of the confusion this could cause:

> Never have people been at such pains to tell from the habit where the highest honours belong. For today we see not only gentlemen but people of low degree wearing embroidery and other adornments which were formerly the prerogative of princes or at least of the most noble lords.

Socially ambitious men and women strove to make an impression by adorning their bodies with colourful and beautiful clothes and jewellery – and by applying perfume – because their actual bodies were less than attractive to smell or look at. They seldom bathed or washed their hair. Only the wealthy indulged in the luxury of separate night attire; most people slept in their basic undergarment, a chemise, which probably did not get washed very often. Everyone, high and low, suffered from fleas and lice. There was, therefore, every incentive to 'cover up' dirty and smelly bodies. And, of course, houses were draughty, which gave people another reason for wearing several layers of clothes.

As well as the unisex chemise, everyone wore 'hose' or long stockings – coarse woollen affairs for the majority and finer garments knitted from wool or silk thread for the better-off. Women wore one or more petticoats and over these a kirtle, a simple, sleeveless, ankle-length dress. Again, this would be of wool unless the wearer could afford finer fabric. The sleeves were separate and pinned or tied to the kirtle. This allowed for the possibility of 'mix-and-match' variation. We know that Henry VIII fell for the charms of a court lady who wore 'Greensleeves'. Workaday women topped the ensemble off with an apron to prevent their dress being soiled. A simple linen cap (coif) kept their hair tidy and moderately clean.

The court ladies of Henry VIII's reign who set the fashion wore several layers of woollen, velvet, silk and fur garments. As well as making them attractive this indicated that they did not do any manual work. These re-enactors are employed at Hampton Court by Past Pleasures Ltd.

Men covered their modesty with 'braes' or baggy underpants, and over these wore loose breeches reaching to the knee. The upper body was covered with a belted leather jerkin. Some men went to the expense of a quilted doublet. For extra warmth a man might wear a short cloak or a longer riding cloak. Also available was the cassock, a long topcoat favoured by older men and those whose work did not depend on great freedom of movement. On his head a man might wear a flat cap, with perhaps a feather or badge attached for bravado.

Beyond these basics fashion took over. Style was set by the royal court, which, in turn, was influenced by the foreign, trend-setting courts of France, Spain and Italy. Every upwardly mobile family moved heaven and earth to place a son or daughter in the king's or queen's household. For this it was vital to equip the young person with an impressive wardrobe. They might, and often did, mortgage whole estates to

This figure of a gaoler shows basic male dress – hose, breeches, doublet and leather jerkin.

buy costumes of brocade and velvets studded with gems. A lady's shape was enhanced by a corset and a farthingale. The latter was a hooped skirt which made her overgown stand out and also accentuated her slim waist. The overgown, of rich silk, was parted at the front to reveal the kirtle of a contrasting or complementary colour. Typical outfits of about 1530 are described as follows:

> Above the chemise they wore a handsome petticoat made of some fine silken camlet, and over this came the farthingale of taffeta, white red, etc. Above this the gown of silvered taffeta of embroidery of fine gold wrought with needlework ... Always they wore a cluster of fine feathers, garnished with gold spangles. Their rings, pendants and gold chains were set with precious stones.

Men about town were not to be outdone in such displays of conspicuous consumption.

> The doublet was of cloth of gold or silver, velvet, satin, damask or taffeta ... slashed [i.e. with small slits to reveal under-material of a different colour], with embroidery and accoutrements to match. Ornamental tags of silk in the same colours, gold tags well enamelled, chamarres (long-sleeved cassocks) of cloth of gold, cloth of silver and velvet galore; the gowns as rich as those of the ladies; silken girdles the same colour as the doublet, and each with his fine sword at his side, the hilt gilded, the scabbard of velvet ...

Not everyone could afford jewels and furs but a woven hat band and a rakish feather could be almost as striking. The ruff was beginning to make its appearance by the 1550s.

By the middle of the century the linen ruff had made its appearance as an item of neckware for men and women.

Cosmetics were equally elaborate – and potentially lethal. Women strove to acquire a pale complexion, simulating that of marble busts. To achieve this effect they mixed white lead with vinegar. The paste used to give lips a cherry red hue often contained mercuric sulphide. Belladonna (from deadly nightshade) was applied to the eyes to make them sparkle. To prevent their teeth discolouring people rubbed them with sticks coated with brick dust and honey. This had the effect of scouring the enamel, thus hastening decay.

One reason for this elaborate display was the

desire by the beautiful people to set themselves apart from the (literally) great unwashed. They were contemptuous of the ruddy complexions of country-men and women that we would today consider healthy. Equally offensive to them was the smell of their poorer neighbours. For this reason they went to great lengths to neutralise the odours which assailed their nostrils. They strewed their floors with sweet-smelling herbs and sprayed their beds and other furniture with rosewater. They carried perfumes about with them in 'casting bottles' ready to sprinkle any malodorous person who came before them. The making of perfumes was a major industry and customers were found not only among the privileged class. For instance, the pomander might take the form of a gold, jewel-encrusted container filled with a mixture of exotic, imported herbs and spices or an orange skin stuffed with a sponge soaked in aromatic vinegar.

This lady playing a hurdy-gurdy shows the simple dress of country folk – a kirtle, protected by an apron over a chemise and a light cap for the hair.

We might think of sixteenth-century clothes and unguents as barriers against the contagion of a grimy, disease-ridden world. No-one had a real conception of the connection between cleanliness and health. They vaguely sensed that 'noisome and pestilential airs' might constitute health hazards. That is why they tipped domestic rubbish, including human waste, out into the streets, and avoided lanes known euphemistically as 'Rose Alley', which were commonly used for people to relieve themselves. When plague or other epidemic broke out, those who could do so moved into the country. Every summer the monarch and the royal court went on progress, staying at a succession of country houses. They had to keep on the move because, after a few days, the overfull latrines used by hundreds of courtiers and servants made a place very malodorous.

For the vast majority, however, clothes and other accoutrements were neither status symbols nor 'armour' to shield against contagion. They remained simply necessary coverings to protect against wind and weather and to mark the status and, often, the occupation of the wearer.

The pomander, which held sweet-smelling herbs and spices, took many forms. This is a modern reproduction of a silver pomander. Such were almost essential for anyone in polite society to cover unpleasant smells.

TRANSPORT

'THE HIGHWAYS be cried out upon; every flood makes them impassable.' So one of Thomas Cromwell's agents complained when he wrote from Lincolnshire in February 1539. One reason why few ordinary people ventured far from their own towns and villages was that travel was an uncomfortable and hazardous business. The low, flat fenland of Lincolnshire and adjacent counties was a particularly difficult terrain to cross and the only people who knew the causeways between treacherous areas of waterlogged ground were the 'fen slodgers'. Strangers who ventured into the region without a local guide did so very much at their own peril. It was far from unusual for men and horses travelling in boggy or marshy regions to disappear without trace. But the problem was much more widespread. 'Many common ways … in Kent be so deep and noyous, by wearing and course of water, that people cannot have their carriages, or passages by horses upon or by the same, but to their great pains peril and jeopardy' (Act of Parliament, 1523). 'Highways' were mere tracks whose width was determined only by the amount of traffic they carried. It is not difficult to understand how rapidly road surfaces disintegrated with the wear and tear caused by wagons and horses, not to mention the impact of herds and flocks of cattle and sheep being driven to market.

Each town and village was responsible for the upkeep of roads within its boundary. Those that took their responsibilities seriously gravelled the surface and marked the road edges for a short distance. Leland reported that the town authorities of Oxford were conscientious: 'There is a causeway of stone from Osney to [Hinksey] ferry and in this causeway be divers bridges of planks. For there the stream of Isis breaketh into many armlets'. Not all town councils followed this commendable example. At Keynsham, near Bristol, Leland noted that the fine six-arched stone bridge was 'all in ruin'. There were no signposts and habitations were few and far between so

Opposite:
The horse litter – seen here in a French manuscript illumination of the fifteenth century – was the least uncomfortable way for ladies and elderly people to travel.

it was very easy for travellers to lose their way, especially if they lost patience with the road conditions and tried to find their own way across country.

But deep ruts, mud and broken bridges were not the only hazards facing travellers. Vagabond gangs constituted a major problem. An Italian visitor in 1500 reckoned 'there is no country in the world where there are so many thieves and robbers as in England'. While we have to be careful about accepting the anecdotal reports of foreigners, there is no doubt that people setting out on long journeys travelled with armed servants or banded together in groups whenever possible. Not that there was always safety in numbers, as another contemporary recounted. 'It hath often been seen in England that three or four thieves, for poverty, hath set upon seven or eight true men and robbed them all. There be more men hanged in England in a year for robbery and manslaughter than there be hanged in France for such cause of crime in seven years', the same visitor reported. Wooded areas, such as Epping and Sherwood forests were particularly notorious.

Towns and cities were self-contained and security-conscious. Many, like this north German example, were walled, with gates that were guarded and closed at night.

The growth of trade and the increasing volume of business conducted by the Crown made reform of the road system a matter of urgency. Yet it was only slowly that central government began to get to grips with the problem. Long tradition had left highway maintenance almost entirely to municipal authorities and private charity. It was a London merchant, John Plot, whose bequest was

Blacksmiths were greatly in demand in Tudor England.

obviously based on first hand experience. He left £5 'to be spendith between London and Ware, of foul ways ... there most need is'. Not until 1531 did the Statute of Bridges empower local magistrates to levy a special rate for the upkeep of bridges. It was another quarter of a century before similar legislation was enacted with regard to roads. The Act of 1555 authorised justices of the peace (JPs) to impress (forcibly co-opt) labourers, together with their tools and wagons, for work on the highways.

One trade that did profit from the bad state of the roads was blacksmithing. Wayside smithies were almost as common as petrol stations are today. There were always cast-off horseshoes to be replaced and broken-down carts to be repaired. Many vehicles had spikes attached to their wheels for better grip. Whatever advantage they gave the wagoners, they certainly did nothing to improve the road surfaces. The situation was much the same within towns.

> All the streets are so badly paved that they get wet at the slightest quantity of water and this happens very frequently owing to the large number of cattle ... as well as the rain ... Then a vast amount of evil-smelling mud is formed which does not disappear quickly ...

This was one visitor's impression of London, where the main thoroughfares were better maintained than in several other towns and cities. Some streets were paved or cobbled and many had a central drainage ditch but this easily became clogged. The responsibility for cleaning the streets was placed on the shoulders of householders, who were expected to keep clear the space outside their premises. But this

The sight of sheep and cattle being driven through towns was very common – even in London. These animals are on their way to Eastcheap market.

Inns where travellers could stay on long journeys or pilgrimages were numerous. Several survive and now look very picturesque. In Tudor times the accommodation they offered was often very basic. This inn, the Tabard in Southwark, was the starting point of the pilgrims in Chaucer's *Canterbury Tales*. It was destroyed in the nineteenth century.

was difficult to enforce and municipal authorities found it necessary to take a hand. Southampton may have been the first town to appoint its own paviour, paid for by a household rate (1482) and in 1501 Nottingham paid a man 33s 4d per year to 'make and mend all the defaults in all places of the said town in the pavements'.

By far the least uncomfortable way to travel long distances was on horseback. Given a road that had not disintegrated into a quagmire, a fit horse could cover about thirty miles a day, which meant that a rider could reach Oxford or Cambridge from London in about two days. Clothiers transported their bales of cloth across country by packhorse trains, which were faster and better over rough ground than wagons. However, it was only merchants, nobles, gentlemen and those whose work involved frequent travel who could afford to keep a stable of horses. For occasional journeys men used a hackney service. The traveller picked up his mount from a dealer (often an innkeeper) and then sold it again when he reached his journey's end. This was a

THE ENCAMPMENT OF THE ENGLISH FORCES NEAR PORTSMOUTH, TOGETHER WITH A VIEW OF THE ENGLISH AND FRENCH FLEETS AT THE COMMENCEMENT OF THE ACTION BETWEEN THEM ON THE XIX OF JULY MDXLV.

particularly useful arrangement for anyone travelling abroad, so that horse-trading businesses thrived at the major ports. Horse travel increased rapidly throughout the early Tudor period. One observer in the 1560s counted 2,200 packhorses during a single journey between London and Enfield. Alongside the hackney system ran the post-horse service. This was designed to provide relays of better, faster horses for conveying letters and urgent messages. Henry VIII set up the first royal post-horse service in 1511. Just how vital this was was demonstrated in October 1536, when the Lincolnshire rebellion broke out. Messengers from Louth, riding hell-for-leather overnight reached the court at Westminster – some 150 miles away – in nine hours.

Ladies, the elderly and the infirm who required a more sedate form of transport had themselves conveyed by horse litter. This was a kind of box supported on each side by long poles attached to the harness of two horses, one at the front and one at the rear. The lead horse was ridden by a groom to ensure that the conveyance proceeded at a steady and safe pace. It must have been a frustratingly slow way of getting about but it was more dignified than travelling in a cart and more comfortable than going by carriage. The litter was at its best on state occasions when fine ladies wanted to be seen progressing in style. Archbishop Cranmer described how Queen Anne Boleyn arrived on such an occasion: 'We received the queen apparelled in a robe of purple velvet … she sitting in her chair upon a horse litter richly apparelled and four knights of the five ports [Cinque Ports] bearing a canopy over her head'. Carriages were in their infancy. They were known, somewhat euphemistically, as 'chariots' and were little more than covered wagons slung on chains – a primitive form of suspension. They must have lurched and shuddered their way horrendously over England's rutted roads.

The sea was vital to English transportation as well as defence. This print shows the French attack on the English fleet at Portsmouth in 1545, at the moment when the great warship *Mary Rose* had just sunk, with sailors floundering in the sea. Henry VIII and his army are visible in the foreground.

EDUCATION

'THIS CHILD HERE, waiting at table … will prove a marvellous man.' According to his biographer, this prophecy was made about the young Thomas More by his patron, Cardinal Morton, while he was serving as a page in that great man's household. More's early career serves as a good example for considering the changing patterns of learning in early Tudor England. More, the son of a City lawyer, began his formal education, when he was probably seven or eight, at St Anthony's school in Threadneedle Street. Like most schools, St Anthony's was an almonry school, attached to a religious foundation. In the Middle Ages the church had held a monopoly of education because learning and literacy were considered as necessary principally for those pursuing an ecclesiastical career. The words 'clerk' and 'cleric' were synonymous. It was men trained for the church who served as administrators and scholarly advisers in noble

Opposite:
This Italian painting of about 1500 depicts an allegory of wisdom opening the door to a child which could allow him to ascend all the levels of the academic syllabus, or *quadrivium*.

This engraving of Thomas More and his family in 1526 is after a lost original by Hans Holbein. More, who was Lord Chancellor to Henry VIII and a friend of the great humanist Erasmus, was devoted to learning, as is shown by the number of books in the picture. He even had his daughters educated, which was unusual at the time.

and royal households. Almonry schools were usually found alongside monasteries and chantry chapels. Monasteries kept schools for the benefit of their choirboys and these were usually open to the sons of the gentry. Chantry priests were able to augment the meagre stipends they obtained for saying masses for wealthy patrons by giving lessons to local boys. St Anthony's was a 'hospital', one of a number of charitable institutions set up for the care of the elderly. As with chantries, the clergy were able to put their knowledge of Latin to good use, in their case by teaching the sons of rich London merchants.

Schools obviously varied greatly in quality. The headmaster of a monastic school might be a university graduate with an extensive knowledge of the Church Fathers and even classical literature. Many a chantry priest, on the other hand, had scarcely enough Latin to be worth passing on to a younger generation. St Anthony's had an excellent reputation largely because it had to compete with four other similar establishments in the City. The pattern of instruction was the same in all these schools. It was based on the *trivium* – the three subjects, Latin grammar (hence the alternative name 'grammar school'), logic and rhetoric. The boys sat on benches or on the floor and listened to the teacher reciting texts which they had to write in their books and learn by rote. The master's birch was always on hand to encourage the more laggard students. Every 23 August, St Bartholomew's Eve, the pupils of the leading London schools came together for a public 'disputation' or debating competition and the boys of St Anthony's were generally recognised by their rivals as the ones to be beaten.

Not all of those who entered this traditional treadmill had a church career in mind. Latin was the international language of scholars and diplomats as well as religious ritual and, therefore, gave entry to wide circles of influence. The grammar school boy might go on to spend some time at university (though not necessarily to take a degree). He might be pointed in the direction of one of the non-ecclesiastical professions – medicine or law. He might aspire to enter the service of the king or of some great nobleman as a steward, magistrate or diplomat. A grammar school education set his foot on the first rung of the preferment ladder.

The fifteenth and sixteenth centuries were a time of foundation of many schools and colleges. Christ Church, Oxford, was founded by Cardinal Wolsey in 1525 as Cardinal College, then refounded in 1532 as King Henry VIII's College.

Other avocations called for different training. Gentlemen and nobles had their sons brought up in other fine households – preferably the royal court. Visitors found this custom strange. 'The want of affection in the English is strongly manifested towards their children,' a Venetian diplomat observed, 'for they put them out, both males and females, to hard service in the houses of other people'. Merchants had the apprentice system prescribed by their guild or livery company. Thomas More was rather unusual in that he sampled different forms of tutelage. From his school he went, at about twelve or thirteen, to the household of Cardinal Morton, Archbishop of Canterbury. In Morton's palace at Lambeth and his various country residences More learned the art and etiquette of gracious living. He served at table, carried messages, attended to the needs of the cardinal's guests and helped to pack the cardinal's silver and gold plate into iron-bound coffers whenever the archiepiscopal household was on the move. The objective of placing Thomas More with such an influential patron was to introduce him to high society and advance his career. It was Morton who procured the boy a place at Oxford, whither More went at the age of fourteen.

At the university he progressed to the next stage of academic education, the *quadrivium* – arithmetic, music, geometry and astronomy. Here he experienced the life common to all students at all ages, a combination of hard study and convivial company. He would have liked to have continued to crown his studies with theology, the 'queen of the sciences', but his father had designated him for a legal career so that, after a couple of years, he returned to London to join one of the inns of court. These 'colleges' for the study of law were clustered together between Holborn and Fleet Street, with the City, England's commercial heart, to the East and Westminster, where government and the law courts were to be found, to the West. Just as the universities were not restricted to those studying for degrees and heading for a professional or academic career, so the inns of court were not the sole preserve of trainee lawyers. Gentlemen and nobles sent their sons there for a few terms to learn the social graces and to pick up enough law to help them manage their estates and to serve as provincial magistrates. More, however, stuck to his last. At New Inn, one of the inns of Chancery, he received his grounding in the judicial system, before proceeding to Lincoln's Inn to become versed in the finer and more contentious points of civil law. By 1501 he was able to set up in practice for himself. There could never have been a better time to be a member of the legal profession. As Erasmus observed, 'there is no better way to eminence than the study of English law'. Henry VII and Henry VIII, both intent on keeping in check the aristocracy of church and state, relied increasingly on the lawyers, who had no other loyalty than to the Crown.

As the new century opened revolutionary changes were transforming the education system. More had passed through it just too early to feel their full effect, although he was excited by the new ideas brought back by *avant garde* thinkers from Renaissance Italy. Greek and Hebrew began to be taught in the universities and students were encouraged to study the Bible in its original languages rather than through the glosses of generations of theologians. John Colet was the leading light of what sneering critics were soon calling the 'new learning'. His lectures on the sacred text had an exhilarating freshness. His scorn for 'scholasticism', the traditional teaching method, excited his young listeners. Colet taught for a while at Oxford and then became Dean of St Paul's Cathedral. In 1510 he established there a new school. His intentions became clear when he appointed as trustees, not the cathedral chapter, but the Mercers' Company because, as he said, he found 'less corruption in such a body of citizens than in any other order or degree of mankind'.

John Colet (1467–1519), Dean of St Paul's, championed a whole new approach to learning, often in the face of much opposition.

John Colet Dean of Sᵗ Paul's

Colet thought through from scratch the whole process of educating the young. He divided his charges into age groups, each with its own master. He banished the arid business of learning grammatical rules, insisting that, by growing familiarity with the best classical authors, students would 'imbibe' vocabulary, syntax and style. His motivation in setting up the school was not improving the standards of the clergy or the education of gentlemen's sons but providing children with something which was valuable in itself, an enlightened and sound foundation for life. This was the essence of humanism – and it was truly revolutionary. Colet received much abuse from the religious establishment who accused him of overthrowing the divine ordering of society.

The leading educational thinker of the next generation was the Spanish humanist Juan Luis Vives (1492–1540), who spent some time in England before falling foul of Henry VIII by opposing his divorce from Catherine of Aragon. In his book, *On the Right Method of Instruction for Children*, Vives raised the bar by insisting that schools should be established in every town and funded by the municipal authorities. Their objective should be, he outrageously suggested, not dinning into young minds a fixed curriculum, but in 'discovering individual inclinations and abilities'. Although Vives had a considerable influence, some of his ideas were well in advance of his time.

The clash of widely differing educational theories created an atmosphere of confusion. This was made worse by the Dissolution of the Monasteries. Reformers who backed the government moves against 'papistical superstition' urged that some of the proceeds should be allocated to founding new schools. They were disappointed; virtually all the money raised from the sale of religious lands and buildings was poured into the deep pit of government debt. Among the casualties were several almonry schools. However, in the brief reign of Edward VI (1547–52) enormous strides were taken towards establishing a nationwide school system. The government set the pace by endowing what became known as King Edward VI schools. Numerous local guilds and town corporations either set up new schools or ensured that old chantry or abbey schools survived.

Education was now a high profile issue at most levels of society. What lay at the root of this change in social attitudes was the influence of printing and comparatively cheap books. Knowledge was no longer confined to those seeking an ecclesiastical or professional career. The religious reformers had successfully implanted the principle that learning was valuable to all people, for itself. Now, nobles, gentlemen, merchants and yeomen all wanted their sons to receive a good schooling. 'Education, education, education' was certainly a motto of the men of the Reformation.

Juan Luis Vives (1492–1540) was the leading educational reformer of the age. For a time he was employed by Henry VIII as a tutor for Princess Mary.

LEISURE

WHEN HENRY VIII and his new queen Katharine passed through London on the eve of their coronation in 1509 his cheering subjects saw an athletic, well-set-up, ruddy-complexioned young man who already had a reputation as a fun-loving prince. Those who followed court gossip in the following years enjoyed tales of spectacular entertainments organised by a monarch dedicated to no-expense-spared partying, as he, himself, explained in verse:

Pastime with good company
I love and shall until I die
Grudge who will, but none deny,
So God be pleased this life will I
For my pastime
Hunt, sing and dance,
My heart is set;
All goodly sport
To my comfort
Who shall me let?

The king jousted, hunted, sang, danced, took part in elaborate court masques and impromptu 'disguisings' (fancy dress charades), played real tennis, skittles, cards, bowls and drew the longbow. Some royal activities were semi-public affairs. On one occasion in 1511 the spectators were so excited that several of them invaded the jousting arena to grab souvenirs from the costly horse trappings and even to pluck gold ornaments from the king's own costume.

But if Henry's subjects thought that they were all going to share in a carefree golden age they learned in the very next year that they were mistaken. An Act of Parliament of 1512 decreed that no artisan, husbandman, labourer, fisherman or servant was permitted to play tennis, skittles, bowls, quoits, dice or card games or other 'unlawful'

Opposite:
Hunting was the sport of kings. For as long as his health lasted, Henry VIII hunted almost every day in season. Large areas of country were reserved for kings, nobles and courtiers to indulge this sport. Engraving by Lucas Cranach, c.1550 (detail).

Tournaments consisted of several games, mounted and on foot, designed to hone the military skills of knights. The joust (shown here in a fanciful nineteenth-century illustration) was the most popular spectator sport.

pastimes except at Christmas and even then only under close supervision by their betters. Unrestrained pleasure was, it seems, a royal prerogative.

There were three main reasons for the restrictions (reinforced by fresh legislation in 1542). One was the determination to maintain strict class divisions (such as we have already seen limiting dress and diet codes). Another was the fear of riot which might grow into civil unrest. Football, one of the most popular of all games had long been proscribed: '... nothing but beastly fury and extreme violence from which proceedeth hurt and consequently rancour and malice do remain with them that be wounded.'

Numerous games were played by Tudor citizens. Here we see a form of skittles, shuttlecock (early badminton) and other games played with racquets.

That was Sir Thomas Elyot's verdict on football. The version of this ancient sport played in Tudor England was certainly a no-holds-barred affair, more like mass wrestling than a game of skill. Contests took place traditionally on fixed holy days such as Shrove Tuesday and involved an unlimited number of people. The only connection of this free-for-all with the modern game was the existence of two goals into which participants tried to hurl a ball. The means of achieving this involved kicking, throwing, carrying the ball and using any means whatsoever from preventing the opposition kicking, throwing or carrying the ball. The game was often played between rival villages, might go on from dawn to dusk and end up with no result apart from a tally of broken limbs and heads. For excitement and danger football was the lower-class equivalent of the jousting and tourneys beloved of kings and courtiers.

Real tennis was a game that originated in monastic cloisters, which explains the layout of the court which had a roofed gallery, called a penthouse, within the playing area. Hampton Court has a tennis court built for Henry VIII.

The third reason why so many apparently harmless pursuits were forbidden to all the king's subjects was that, so the government claimed, it distracted people from the one sport the regime wished to encourage – archery. The Tudor monarchs were determined to ensure that they had a large reservoir of men competent in the use of the longbow in case of war. Accordingly every male between the ages of 17 and 60 (with the exception of clergy and judges) were to keep a bow and four arrows and to practise regularly in butts provided by the local authorities. Just as members of the

The crossbow, which was popular for hunting game, was frowned upon by the government. Because of its relatively slow rate of fire it was of less use in warfare and the king wanted his subjects to be proficient in the more effective longbow.

Bear- and bull-baiting were very popular spectator sports and several towns had 'pits' built for this activity.

In his book *The Ship of Fools* the German satirist, Sebastian Brandt, depicted as fools those who played cards for money.

governing class kept up their martial skills in the tiltyard, so their humbler countrymen were expected to be in readiness to serve king and country on the field of battle. War was seldom out of mind for the first two Tudors.

In an age when people turned out to watch public executions and the humiliation of criminals, were quite accustomed to the sight of rotting bodies swinging on gibbets, and considered birching an integral part of educating children it was inevitable that violence should have featured prominently in leisure activities. Hunting and hawking were the favourite pursuits of the king and his companions. When Henry VIII was on progress, as he was for most of every summer, he spent days on end in the hunting field. Back in Westminster he enjoyed cock fighting and had a cockpit built in his palace there. Londoners and visitors to the capital delighted at bear baiting, which they could witness in a purpose-built 'pit' on the south bank of the Thames at Southwark (after they had passed across London Bridge where the heads of decapitated felons were displayed on poles). Henry VIII was among those who enjoyed this spectacle and sometimes had events arranged at court for the delight of himself and his guests. For this pastime a beast (they still existed in the wild in England) was chained to a stake to restrict its movements and dogs were then set on it, while the onlookers wagered on how many hounds would survive and which would deliver the *coup de grâce*. Bull-baiting was a more common spectacle, since the animals destined to be tormented were more readily available. The bull was tethered with a five-yard rope attached to its horns. Pepper was often blown into its nostrils to make it angry. Then trained bulldogs were set upon it one at a time, the prize going to the first to bite the bull's snout. Owners took bets on the prowess of their animals.

Gambling was, as always, popular and, as always, a mugs' game. In Sebastian Brandt's painting *Ship of Fools* people who got themselves embroiled in games of chance were depicted dressed in jesters' motley. Playing cards, introduced to the country sometime in the fifteenth century, seem to have reached all levels of society by the beginning of the Tudor period. After a day in the hunting field and an evening's dancing, Henry VIII, an enthusiastic gamesman, often sat up till late in the night, playing at dice or cards. The King appears not have been the best of losers. On one occasion in 1511 some Italian bankers took a lot of money off him at dice, whereupon he accused them of cheating and threw them out. We know the names of several Tudor card games – gleek, new cut, primero – but their rules are elusive. However, the fact that so many variants existed indicates just how popular this pastime was, whether indulged in by polite family groups or more dubious alehouse company.

However, the basic 'pleasure routine' was that bound up with the festivals of the church and even older pagan survivals. Shrove Tuesday, Easter, May Day, Whitsun, Christmas, saints' days and other fixtures in the festive calendar all provided opportunities for merrymaking. Every parish had its own way of marking these red-letter days. Each May Day the churchwardens of Kingston-on-Thames provided costumes and props for 'Robin Hood … the friar, Maid Marian … and Littler John'. The separate stories of these stock characters of popular legend were brought together for the first time in the early Tudor period. Together with Morris dancers they enacted various scenes: buffoonery, mock heroism and bawdy. More serious were the mystery plays performed on Corpus Christi Day in late May or early June. A procession of pageant wagons passed through the streets and on each one members of the local guilds enacted scenes based – often loosely – on major biblical events. These equivalents of the more sophisticated dramas performed at the courts of kings and nobles broke up the monotony of rural and urban life and people flocked to them. They even turned up eagerly to hear what wandering friars had to say when they stood up to preach by the market cross.

Traditionally, major church festivals were marked by morality plays. One of the more popular was *Everyman*. the script of which was published in 1509 (title page shown here). It reminded audiences that they would be judged after death according to their deeds.

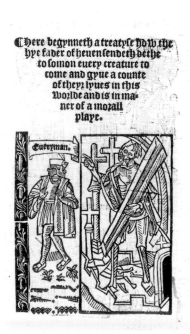

Serratura.

HEALTH

SIXTEENTH-CENTURY people lived close to death. The average life expectancy was 35. A few people lived into what we would now consider as old age but the more vulnerable members of society died young, children especially. Probably a quarter of babies did not reach the age of five. People succumbed to a variety of ills and afflictions which would not be terminal today. A fractured leg might turn septic because there was no understanding of simple clinical hygiene. That might necessitate surgery. The only anaesthesia available consisted of the dangerous drugs opium and hemlock – which sometimes killed before the surgeon's knife came anywhere near the damaged limb – and alcohol. Therefore, the patient faced the operation in a state of complete or semi-consciousness and was tied or held down to stop him moving. If the shock did not prove fatal, post-operative gangrene often did. Childbirth was particularly hazardous. Henry VII's wife, Elizabeth of York, and Henry VIII's third queen, Jane Seymour, were

Opposite: Surgery was primitive, painful and often fatal. Here a leg is amputated without benefit of anaesthetic.

Hans Holbein, who was court painter to Henry VIII, designed a series of engravings entitled *The Dance of Death* to remind people that death strikes equally at people of all classes, nobles as well as ploughmen.

Trained physicians were rare and expensive. Many people had recourse to quacks. This woodcut exposes a charlatan. His licence to practise is labelled *mendax* – 'liar' – and the Latin inscription warns the sick to shun danger.

just two of the thousands of women who died from post-natal complications.

Numerous diseases haunted the unsanitary homes of the poorer members of society. 'Plague', a word used to describe a variety of contagions, was not as devastating at this time as it was in its fourteenth- and seventeenth- century visitations, but it was seldom absent. 'They have some little plague in England well nigh every year,' a Venetian ambassador reported. 'The cases for the most part occur amongst the lower classes, as if their dissolute mode of life impaired their constitutions.' Other familiar diseases were syphilis and typhus. Both were studied and described by the Italian writer, Hieronymus Fracastorius, in his *De Contagione* (1546) but contemporary medicine was not equipped to follow diagnosis with effective treatment. Mercury was believed to be efficacious in the treatment of syphilis, which led to the saying, 'A night in the arms of Venus leads to a lifetime on Mercury'.

The two most feared diseases were recent arrivals – smallpox and the sweating sickness. The former was fatal in, perhaps, fifty per cent of cases and those who recovered were often horribly scarred. The sweating sickness is believed to have arrived in England with Henry VII's army in 1485 and reappeared at irregular intervals until 1551, after which it disappeared. Unlike other infections, it could strike anyone, anywhere; dwellers in town or country, hovel or palace. People called it 'Stoop-knave-and-know-thy-master'. Victims suffered from high temperature, headache, thirst and an overwhelming desire to sleep (which had to be avoided at all costs). It could kill in three hours. Henry VIII, who was something of a hypochondriac, was terrified of it. The year 1528 saw a particularly virulent outbreak. The king was staying at Tyttenhanger, near St Albans, when he learned that, 'my Lady Marquis of Exeter is sick of the common sickness'. He immediately set out for Ampthill 'and hath commanded that all such as were in my said Lord Marquis's company and my said Lady [are] to depart in several parcels and not to continue together'. Malaria and related fevers were rampant. A long spell in a damp, airless gaol such as London's Newgate or the Fleet was virtually a death sentence.

Treatment for syphilis, a new disease in Europe in the sixteenth century. A doctor examines his female patient's urine while his assistant applies mercuric ointment to her husband.

People suffering from ill health had recourse to a wide range of medical practitioners. In 1518 those who had studied their craft at university founded the College of Physicians in order to exclude such 'common artificers as smiths, weavers and women who boldly and customarily take upon themselves great cures … in which they use sorcery and apply medicines very noyous'. Among the quacks who preyed upon the sick were 'wise women' who concocted herbal remedies, alchemists who made up all manner of weird potions and sorcerers who relied on spells and incantations. To most observers these amateurs seemed little different

Herbal remedies were important in the treatment of disease. Some people kept gardens for the cultivation of efficacious plants.

The great German artist, Albrecht Dürer, was one of several who illustrated in lurid detail the 'Day of Wrath' which many people feared was imminent.

from the professionals, for they relied on casting horoscopes as well as prescribing medicines.

Because life was transitory, people could readily believe that the planet also was hurrying towards its doom. Around the beginning of the century there was much talk of the Last Judgement bursting upon a sinful world, and every natural disaster seemed to many to herald the destruction of the natural order prophesied in the New Testament's Book of Revelation. Various apocalyptic groups preaching the imminent end of the world appeared on the Continent at frequent intervals and England was not without its crop of wild-eyed visionaries. It was fear of a wrathful God and familiarity with death which impelled many people to seek the ministrations of the Church. Traditional Catholic doctrine taught that everyone would have to face Christ on the Day of Judgement and be consigned to heaven or hell. Until then the departed soul had to spend time in purgatory to purge itself of sins committed in this life. The time spent in this 'half-way house' could be determined by the prayers of those left behind and, particularly, by the granting of 'indulgences', authorised by the pope. These released the soul from varying terms in purgatory. No-one could know in advance what his or her fate would be in the next world, so one could only trust in the rites of holy Church. Imagine, then, the impact on traditional believers when the ideas of the German reformer Martin Luther began to circulate in the 1520s. He taught (in 1517) that indulgences were a fraud and that, according to the Bible, there was no such thing as purgatory. Church leaders condemned Luther and those who followed his teaching as heretics. Several people were burned at the stake during the reigns of Henry VIII and Mary Tudor for following him. But an increasing number of people, especially among

During the reigns of Henry VIII and Mary Tudor hundreds of Protestants were burned at the stake in London's Smithfield for denying the teaching of the Catholic Church. A sermon was preached as crowds watched the martyrs' grisly end.

Whatever official religion held sway, superstition was still rife. Here witches are shown conjuring up a hailstorm.

the literate class who could read Luther's books for themselves, believed in what came to be known as Protestantism. Their new style of Christianity, which was confirmed as the national orthodoxy during the reign of Henry VIII's son Edward VI, differed profoundly from the old. It was not just that images, paintings and coloured windows disappeared; also purged was a religion based on a priestcraft and the 'miracle' of the mass (according to which the bread and wine were believed literally to become the body and blood of Christ). The new faith was individual, rational and based on a vernacular Bible that all were encouraged to read for themselves. Above all, it offered what the old had never been able to provide – certainty of salvation.

But not everyone was committed to the Protestant Reformation. Long-established customs and beliefs lingered. Not just medieval Catholicism: witchcraft, necromancy, magic, scepticism and a range of eccentric, personal religious variations survived. They had always been there. They would be there for generations to come. In this age of revolutionary change not all things changed at the same pace.

PLACES TO VISIT

NATIONAL TRUST SITES
For National Trust sites, go to www.nationaltrust.org.uk and search for the
relevant house.

Fountains Abbey, Ripon Nr Harrogate, North Yorkshire, HG4 3DY
   The Cistercian monastery, one of hundreds dissolved by Henry VIII in
   the 1530s, now a picturesque ruin.

Paycocke's, Coggeshall, Essex, CO6 1NS
   A house built around 1500, which features elaborate panelling and
   carvings, a testament to the wealth generated by the wool trade.

Sutton House, Hackney, London, 2 & 4 Homerton High St, Hackney,
   London E9 6JQ
   Built in 1535 by Sir Ralph Sadlier, this is a rare red-brick Tudor house,
   with original panelling and many other features.

Lacock Abbey, Lacock, nr Chippenham, Wiltshire SN15 2LG
   Medieval abbey dissolved in 1539 and converted to private use, with
   Tudor and later features.

Cotehele, St Dominick, nr Saltash, Cornwall PL12 6TA
   A well preserved and little altered house built 1485-1539, with fine
   tapestries and great hall.

Packwood House, Packwood Lane, Lapworth, Warwickshire B94 6AT
   Oak-panelled house built in the mid-sixteenth century.

Rufford Old Hall, 200 Liverpool Road, Rufford, nr Ormskirk, Lancashire
   L40 1SG
   One of Lancashire's finest Tudor buildings, famed for its great hall with
   an intricately carved moveable wooden screen and hammerbeam roof.

Ightham Mote, Mote Road, Ivy Hatch, Sevenoaks, Kent TN15 0NT
   Fourteenth-century manor house with a magnificent great hall, crypt,
   and Tudor Chapel with a hand-painted ceiling, decorated with symbols
   of Henry VIII and Catherine of Aragon.

Oxburgh Hall, King's Lynn, Norfolk PE33 9PS
   A moated manor house with a magnificent Tudor gatehouse.

Lytes Cary Manor, nr Charlton Mackrell, Somerton, Somerset TA11 7HU
   Medieval manor with fine great hall, sixteenth-century additions and
   Jacobean furniture.

OTHERS
Hampton Court Palace, Surrey, KT8 9AU
   Website www.hrp.org.uk/HamptonCourtPalace

Henry VIII's finest palace, with his great hall, apartment, tennis court, chapel royal and a collection of royal portraits.

Tower of London, London, EC3N 4AB

www.hrp.org.uk/TowerOfLondon

The scene of many dramatic events, while the White Tower contains an unrivalled collection of armour including Henry VIII's own.

Museum of London, London Wall, London, EC2Y 5HN

www.museumoflondon.org.uk

Museum with a fine Tudor gallery covering many aspects of life including metal artefacts, dress, weaponry, ceramics, glass and more.

Lavenham church and village, Suffolk. The village boasts fine late medival timber-framed houses; the church is one of the last great Suffolk churches, in Perpendicular style, completed about 1530.

Mary Rose Museum, Portsmouth, PO1 3LX

A time-capsule of life in the 1540s, the museum contains thousands of objects recovered from the seabed after the King's flagship sank in 1545. A new museum is shortly to be built.

Hever Castle, Hever, Nr Edenbridge, Kent TN8 7NG

The childhood home of Anne Boleyn, with a fine collection of Tudor interiors, tapestries and furniture, enlivened by costumed interpreters.

Haddon Hall, Bakewell, Derbyshire DE45 1LA

www.haddonhall.co.uk

Stately home dating back to the early medieval period but with significant Tudor elements.

Kentwell Hall, Suffolk, Long Melford, Suffolk, CO10 9BA

www.kentwell.co.uk

Tudor moated manor house, mainly built 1500-50, which today houses a large and thoroughly researched Tudor Life Recreation each summer.

St Mary's House and Gardens, Bramber, West Sussex, BN44 3WE

www.stmarysbramber.co.uk

A fine timber-framed house built in the 1470s with a Tudor and Jacobean interior.

Louth Church, Louth, Lincolnshire LN11 6ET

www.stjameschurchlouth.com

Completed in 1515, it has the highest spire in England, and the scene of rebellion in 1536.

St Mawes Castle, St Mawes,, Cornwall

www.stmawes.info

One of a chain of circular castles built by Henry VIII to defend the south coast against attack.

INDEX